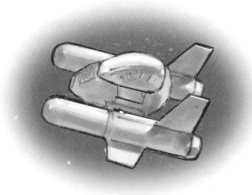

By Lael Littke

Illustrated by Jon Davis

Dominie Press, Inc.

Publisher: Raymond Yuen
Project Editor: John S. F. Graham
Editor: Bob Rowland
Designer: Greg DiGenti
Illustrator: Jon Davis

Published by:

ₚₑ Dominie Press, Inc.

1949 Kellogg Avenue
Carlsbad, California 92008 USA

www.dominie.com

1-800-232-4570

Paperback ISBN 0-7685-2065-7
Printed in Singapore
16 17 18 V0ZF 14

Table of Contents

Chapter One
The Junior Space Race

Tamra parked her little red space car and walked to the building with the long banner over its door.

JUNIOR SPACE RACE, the banner said. *AGES 8 TO 12*. Then the date, *June 5, 2057*.

Tamra took a deep breath before opening the door. This race was very important to her. She was the youngest person to take part, but she planned to win it.

"Hi, Shorty," yelled Dirk as Tamra walked into the large room where the rest of the racers waited in their space suits. "Since when do they let babies like you enter a space race?"

A lot of kids laughed. Some of them repeated, "Hi, Shorty."

"Somebody turn off the sun," Dirk yelled. "We can use little Tamra's red hair and freckles for light out in space."

Tamra just smiled. Dirk would be sorry when she beat him in the race.

A loud voice said, "Attention all racers. Please pick an animal name for yourself.

This is what you'll be called in the race."

Dirk yelled out his animal name first. "*Space Tiger*," he said.

"*Space Shark*," a girl called.

Everybody chose names of big, scary animals. One boy even chose *Space Dragon*.

When it was Tamra's turn, she didn't try to think of a scary animal. She picked a little, unimportant one. "*Space Slug*," she called.

She was going to ace this race and show everybody that even little unimportant people can be winners.

Could she really do it?

Chapter Two
Catch Me If You Can

Tamra had never won anything before in her whole life. But she could make her little red space car do amazing things. That should be enough to win the race.

"Attention all racers," the loud voice shouted. "It is time to launch. When everyone is out in space, we will fire a flare to begin the race. The first thing you must do is fly three circles around Asteroid 57, and then go on to the next asteroid."

Tamra hurried outside with the other racers. She got into her little red space car and put on her space helmet.

Soon it was her turn to launch.

Just before she zoomed off into space, Tamra waved to her mom and dad, who were watching. They would be proud of her when she won.

Out in space, Tamra found she was right next to Dirk. His space car was orange with black stripes, like a tiger. It looked like Dirk had spent a lot of time painting it.

When Dirk saw Tamra, he waved.

Then he put his hand over his eyes as if her red hair and freckles were too bright to look at.

"Catch me if you can, little *Space Slug*," he yelled to her over the spacecraft radio.

Tamra waved back. She would catch him, all right.

Suddenly she saw a flare, which meant

the race was beginning. *Oh, no!* It was too soon. She'd been thinking about beating Dirk and wasn't ready.

She saw Dirk race off ahead of her.

Chapter Three
Too Close

Tamra was right behind Dirk all the way to Asteroid 57. Maybe she could get ahead when they did their circles around it.

Dirk must have been nervous about having Tamra so close, because he made his circles too small. This was dangerous.

If he got too close to the asteroid, its gravity could pull him down.

"Be careful, *Space Tiger*," Tamra said over the radio. But Dirk just laughed.

He did his circles without any problems. Now he was even farther ahead of Tamra.

Next, the racers had to do a figure eight around Asteroid 72. This was hard because the asteroid was big. In the practice sessions some kids had to slow down to do it. Tamra had practiced until she could do it full speed. She was sure she could catch up with Dirk there.

He was still ahead when they got to the big asteroid. But Tamra was close to him. The other racers were far behind.

Tamra made her little space car go faster. Now she was right on the tail of Dirk's tiger-striped space car.

Dirk went faster, too. Tamra saw him

dive very close to the asteroid, probably
to shorten the distance of his figure eight.

Quickly she switched on her radio.
"*Space Tiger*," she yelled. "You're going
in too far and too fast."

"What's the matter, *Space Slug*?" Dirk
said. "Are you afraid?"

All of a sudden his space car spun out
of control. It was caught in the asteroid's
gravity.

Chapter Four
Dead Space

Tamra watched Dirk's space car plunge toward the big asteroid. Looking down, she saw that its surface was all jagged peaks and rocky valleys.

"*Space Tiger*!" Tamra called over the radio. "Turn toward the sun and slam on full power."

But the tiger-striped space car continued to fall.

"I guess you're going to win, little *Space Slug*," Dirk yelled. "I have to land."

Land? *Crash* was more like it.

It was his own fault. They'd been told in practice sessions to stay far enough out in space so they wouldn't get caught in the gravity of the asteroids. Dirk had ignored all the warnings.

"I'll call the rescue ship," Tamra told him. Dirk would be OK if the rescue ship came soon.

Now Tamra knew she would win the race. She was ahead of all the other racers.

She pressed a button to call for help. She would tell the rescue ship where to find Dirk.

"Emergency," she yelled. "*Space Tiger*

is in trouble. He's going down."

But all she heard was a crackle over the radio. Her message wasn't getting through.

It was then Tamra realized she and Dirk were in a dead space behind the asteroid. There was no way to call the rescue ship.

Had any of the other racers seen Dirk's space car go down?

Chapter Five
The Rescue Ship

Tamra knew that if she hung around very long, the other racers would fly past her. She would lose the race.

But Dirk was in trouble. Tamra could see him. He stood on a rocky peak beside the wreckage of his space car. He wore his space suit and helmet.

He was OK. The rescue ship would find him as soon as Tamra was able to call them.

But how? The asteroid was big. They might spend so much time looking for him that the air in his space suit would run out.

Tamra knew now what she must do. She pushed more buttons on her radio. "This is *Space Slug*," she said. "Can anybody hear me?"

"This is *Space Shark*," a voice said through her earphones. "I'm very close behind you. Do you have a problem?"

Quickly Tamra explained what had happened. "Call the rescue ship as soon as you get out of the dead space," she instructed. "I'll stay here to mark where *Space Tiger* went down."

"You'll be out of the race if you stay here," *Space Shark* said.

"I know," Tamra said. "You go ahead and win it."

"I'll try," *Space Shark* said. "Do you have enough fuel to hang there for a while?"

Tamra hadn't even thought of that. She looked at the fuel gauge. It was very low.

"I hope I have enough," she said.

Chapter Six
True Courage

Tamra watched the fuel gauge of her space car drop lower and lower. But she kept on circling above the spot where Dirk had crashed. She hoped the rescue ship would get there really soon. Where was it?

Her radio crackled. *"Space Slug."* It was Dirk's voice. "Are you still there?"

"Yes," she said. "I'll stay to show the rescue ship where you are."

There was a short silence. Then Dirk said, "Thanks, *Space Slug*. It's scary down here. My radio works, but I can't get through to anybody but you."

Tamra told him they were in a dead space behind the asteroid. "Don't worry," she said. *"Space Shark* will tell the rescue ship. They'll be coming soon."

But would they come soon enough, before her fuel ran out?

The gauge showed that her fuel tank was almost empty. Would she crash, too?

Suddenly she saw the big white rescue ship coming.

"Good job, *Space Slug*," they radioed. "We'll get him now. You finish the race."

What race? It was all over. Sadly, Tamra turned her space car back toward Earth.

She was the very last one to return. But after she landed, she heard everybody cheering. It wasn't until she got out of her space car that she realized they were cheering for her. They had made a huge banner. It said, SPACE SLUG WINS PRIZE FOR TRUE COURAGE.

And when the rescue ship arrived with Dirk, he said, "*Space Slug*, you're the best friend I've ever had!"

All of the other kids cheered again.

Tamra smiled. She'd lost the race, but she'd won something much more important.